To my loving grandson Timmy from Memere L.

I guess you could say I really like the letter **Z**. My name is Zachary and I love to go to the zoo. So does my whole family—Mommy, Daddy, and my little sister, Nicole.

There's a special place called the children's zoo where you can touch the animals, and we go there first. It's so much fun to feed Dunkin. He's a llama and he eats with his lips. That's because llamas don't have any upper front teeth. His keeper, Diane, lets me give him some sweet feed which is made of corn and molasses. It's a treat they give him for being good.

When a llama gets upset, he may spit at you.
But most of the time they're friendly.

Afterward, if Nicole and I have a snack, I pretend
I am a llama.

Lollipop is from the French Alps and she has fun scrambling over the tires. Goats usually live in the mountains, so they're very sure-footed and enjoy climbing.

Whisper is a little black pygmy goat and she comes from Africa.

No matter where they're from, goats will nibble on almost anything. Once, Wookie tried to eat Nicole's teddy bear but she grabbed it away just in time.

Rosy is a boa constrictor—a rainbow boa—and she's almost four feet long. She could be a he, because it's hard to tell if a snake is a boy or a girl. Boas shed their skin as often as six times a year because they're always getting bigger and they grow right out of their clothes. Snakes haven't got eyelids, so they never close their eyes.

Don't ever hug a boa constrictor because it might hug you back. And that could be dangerous!

All of the animals have people who take care of them. They're called zoo keepers and they spend a lot of time with visitors explaining how the different animals behave and why people should respect them.

Whenever Debbie asks me if I wish I could take Rosy home with me, I tell her that I already have a dog named Winston and one pet is all I can handle.

There are two species of elephants—African and Indian. You can tell Mame and Jessie are from Africa because they have big floppy ears.

Elephants are the biggest animals that walk on four legs. Their skin is one inch thick and they're called pachyderms, which means "thick skin."

Elephants use their trunks for drinking and carrying heavy stuff. When they make noise through their trunks it's called trumpeting, and it's very, very loud!

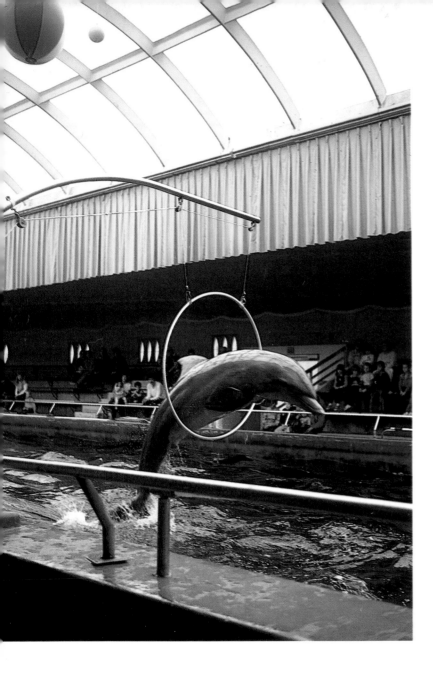

Dolphins are not fish—they're mammals. That means they have to breathe air to survive. But they spend their whole life in the water.

They're very smart and they love to do tricks.

Sometimes the trainer will let Nicole and me say hello to the dolphins after the show is over. We've gone so often that I think they're beginning to know us.

We go to the Aquatic Bird House to see the beautiful pink flamingos. They can stand on one leg for the longest time— much longer than I can.

They love to play follow the leader. They usually walk in a group, and whenever one flamingo changes direction, they all change direction at the exact same time.

Robin is an orangutan, which means "man of the forest." Orangs are not monkeys— they're one of the four great apes. Monkeys have tails and apes don't. But Robin can swing in the trees by using his hands and feet. At night he sleeps in a bed of hay.

The baboons haven't been given names by their keepers because there are so many of them. Even though these monkeys have tails, they don't use them for swinging because they live on the ground.

The snow leopard is so beautiful I could watch it for hours. It's an endangered species, which means there are only a few of them left in the world.

No two zebras are alike—their stripes are always different. They're very shy, and when people come too close they run away.

Giraffes have four stomachs and their tongues are more than a foot long. They sleep standing up or kneeling.

They have very long necks, which makes it possible for them to eat leaves from the tops of trees.

You can tell what part of Africa a giraffe is from by looking at its markings.

Damascus and his mate are from Africa. Everyone calls the lion King of the Jungle, but since he prefers to live in wide-open places it would be better to call him Prince of the Plains.

Polar bears are usually born as twins. The babies weigh about two pounds and they have no fur. Before they're born in the wild, their mother carves a little room out of the snow so they'll stay warm. For them the first big challenge in life is learning how to swim. Their mommy teaches them.

Polar bears are always white and they look cuddly, but they'll bite if you get too close. Uri and Arki love to play in the water, even when it's freezing. Luckily, they have warm fur coats! They just celebrated their first birthday.

We save Olga, the walrus, for last because she's our favorite.
Even though she's a girl, she has whiskers. She weighs about
three thousand pounds and only likes clams, squid, and
mackerel. Olga can wave, whistle, and blow a kiss.

When I get home, I talk to Winston about
all the wonderful animals at the zoo. But
I tell him he'll always be my very best friend.